The Easy-Peasy Gui

By Ava Vintner

Copyright Page

Copyright © 2025 Ava Vintner

All rights reserved. No part of this book may be reproduced, distributed, or transmitted in any form or by any means, including photocopying, recording, or other electronic or mechanical methods, without the prior written permission of the author, except in the case of brief quotations used in reviews and certain other noncommercial uses permitted by copyright law.

This book is intended for educational and entertainment purposes only. The information provided reflects the author's personal research and experience and should not be considered professional advice.

Readers are encouraged to enjoy wine responsibly and in accordance with local laws and regulations. The author and publisher assume no liability for the actions of readers or the outcomes of applying the information contained in this book.

Dedication

For everyone who has ever stared at a wine list and thought,
"I have no idea what I'm looking at."

This book is for you.

Here's to learning, laughing, and finding wines you truly love.

Table of Contents

Introduction: Welcome to the World of Wine 1

Chapter 1 – Wine Without the Snobbery: The Basics You Need to Know 9

    Wine's Rich History – More Than Just a Fancy Beverage 10

    The Three Pillars of Wine Understanding 11

    The Main Wine Styles: Red, White, Rosé, and Sparkling 15

    Sweet vs. Dry: Understanding Wine Sweetness 16

    How Alcohol Content Shapes the Experience 17

    Myth-Busting: Wine Edition 18

    Wrapping Up 19

Chapter 2 – Essential Wine Gear (Without the Gadget Overload) 21

    The Bare Essentials: What You Truly Need 22

    Nice-to-Have Extras 26

    Fun Extras 29

    Avoiding Gadget Overload 30

    Easy Storage Solutions for Small Spaces 31

    Wrapping Up 32

Chapter 3 – Wine 101: How to Read a Bottle Like a Pro 33

    The Key Parts of a Wine Label 34

    Common Wine Terms Made Simple 39

    International Wine Labeling Differences 40

    How to Spot Value Wines 45

Mini-Exercise: Comparing Two Labels 46

Wrapping Up 47

Chapter 4 – Reds, Whites, and Rosés: The Big Categories 49

Red Wines: Bold, Smooth, and Everything In Between 50

White Wines: Crisp, Buttery, or Floral 55

Rosé: More Than Just "Pink Wine" 60

Sparkling Wines: A Touch of Celebration 62

Quick Reference Cheat Sheet 65

Wrapping Up 66

Chapter 5 – How to Taste Wine (Without Feeling Silly) 67

The 5 S's of Wine Tasting 68

Describing What You Taste (Without Sounding Pretentious) . 74

Why "Legs" Don't Really Matter 75

Fun Tasting Game: Blind Wine Challenge 76

Optional Tasting Notes (No Printables Required) 77

Wrapping Up 78

Chapter 6 – Pairing Wine with Food (Simple Rules That Work) 79

The Basic Pairing Principle: Match Intensity 80

Classic Pairings You'll Hear About 81

Why Rules Are Meant to Be Broken 82

Easy Pairing Table for Everyday Foods 83

Fun DIY Wine and Cheese Night 84

Tips for Hosting Without Stress 86

Wrapping Up 87

Chapter 7 – Buying Wine Without Breaking the Bank 89

Understanding Price Tiers 90

Finding Hidden Gems at Grocery Stores and Local Shops 94

The Importance of Asking Staff for Recommendations 97

How to Buy Wine Online Safely 98

Navigating Wine Club Memberships 99

Understanding "House Wines" at Restaurants 100

Fun Challenge: Three Wines Under $15 101

Wrapping Up 102

Chapter 8 – Storing and Serving Wine the Easy Way 103

Ideal Wine Storage Conditions 104

Quick Tips for Those Without a Wine Cellar 108

Serving Temperature Guide 109

How to Revive an "Off" Bottle 111

How Long Wine Lasts After Opening 112

Storing Leftover Wine for Cooking 113

Wrapping Up 114

Chapter 9 – Exploring Wine Regions: Your Virtual Passport .. 115

Old World vs. New World Wines 116

France: A Wine Legacy 119

Italy: Passion and Tradition 123

Spain: Bold and Accessible 126

United States: Innovation and Variety 129

Other Regions to Explore 133

Wrapping It Up: Your Wine Travel Goals 137
Chapter 10 – Becoming a Confident Wine Lover 139
Tracking Your Wine Journey 140
Hosting Wine Nights with Friends 144
Exploring More Advanced Concepts 147
Keeping Wine Fun and Approachable 148
Final Toast: Celebrate Your Progress 149
Wrapping Up the Book 150
Glossary of Wine Terms 151
Quick Tasting Sheet Guide 153
Quick Reference Pairing Chart 154
Resources & Further Reading 155
About the Author 157
Index 158
A Final Note 160

Introduction: Welcome to the World of Wine

Wine is one of those things that tends to carry a certain mystique. Maybe it's the way it's swirled dramatically in oversized glasses in movies, or the endless rows of bottles at the store with labels you can barely pronounce. Perhaps it's the way some people talk about wine as if they've memorized a secret code—throwing around words like "tannins," "mouthfeel," and "terroir." For many beginners, it can all feel a little intimidating.

Here's the good news: wine doesn't have to be complicated. In fact, it shouldn't be. At its core, wine is simply fermented grape juice, a natural product that's been enjoyed for thousands of years by everyday people all over the world. From ancient celebrations to quiet evenings at home, wine has always been about connection, pleasure, and shared experiences.

This book is here to help you cut through the noise and focus on what really matters: learning how to enjoy wine in a way that feels simple and fun. You don't need to memorize every grape variety, know the names of obscure regions, or be able to detect notes of wild truffle and aged leather in your glass. You just need a little guidance and a willingness to explore.

Why Wine Feels So Intimidating

The wine world can seem exclusive because it's full of traditions and specialized terms. Restaurants have sommeliers who speak in what can sound like another language. Certain wines are surrounded by prestige and hefty price tags, giving the impression that only serious connoisseurs can appreciate them.

This mystique has its roots in history. Wine was once a symbol of status, tied to noble families and royal courts. Over time, this sense of prestige was carried forward, and today it still shows up in fancy labels, high-end tastings, and the idea that wine knowledge is reserved for the elite.

The truth is, you don't have to be a collector or a critic to love wine. You don't even need to own a single decanter or have a "wine fridge." Wine is meant to be enjoyed by anyone, whether you're sipping a crisp glass of white while cooking dinner or sharing a bottle of red with friends on the back porch.

What Makes This Book Different

There are plenty of wine books out there, but many of them are packed with technical details or overwhelming charts that can make a beginner's head spin. *The Easy-Peasy Guide to Wine* takes a different approach.

Think of this as a conversation with a trusted friend, the kind of friend who loves wine but doesn't make a big fuss about it. Everything in these pages is straightforward, easy to understand, and completely free of judgment. My goal is to help you feel confident and excited to explore wine, not nervous or self-conscious.

Instead of memorizing facts, you'll be encouraged to discover what *you* like. Along the way, you'll learn practical tips for buying, tasting, and pairing wine without spending a fortune or feeling lost in a maze of options. You'll be able to talk about wine with ease, whether you're ordering at a restaurant or choosing a bottle at the store.

Taste, Experiment, and Enjoy

Wine isn't about rules, it's about personal experience. Part of the fun is tasting different wines and seeing which ones speak to you. Some people love bold, earthy reds, while others gravitate toward light, citrusy whites. There's no wrong answer, and your preferences may evolve over time.

This book will encourage you to experiment. Try wines from regions you've never heard of, pair them with your favorite meals, and notice how different flavors interact. You don't need a perfect palate to start exploring. The more you taste, the more confident you'll become in understanding your own likes and dislikes.

Wine is also about sharing. A bottle opens conversations and creates memories, whether it's a simple weekday dinner or a special celebration. When you approach wine with curiosity and openness, you'll find that it enhances not just the meal, but the entire experience.

What to Expect in the Chapters Ahead

Here's a quick taste of what's to come:
You'll start by learning the very basics of wine—what it is, where it comes from, and why certain types taste the way they do. Then, we'll talk about the simple gear you need, how to read a wine label without confusion, and how to taste wine confidently.

We'll explore pairing wine with food, buying wine on a budget, and storing it properly. You'll also take a virtual journey through some of the world's most famous wine regions, getting to know their unique styles and stories. By the time you reach the end of this book, you'll have a strong foundation for enjoying wine on your own terms.

A Friendly Reminder About Responsible Drinking

As you begin this journey, remember that wine is best enjoyed mindfully and in moderation. Drinking should always be a positive experience, never something that causes harm or regret.
Know your limits, respect local laws, and savor each sip. The goal is to enhance your life and your meals—not to drink simply for the sake of drinking.

A Final Word Before We Begin

You don't have to know anything about wine to start this book, and you don't have to learn everything at once. This is your invitation to step into a world full of flavor, history, and discovery—without the intimidation factor.

So, pour yourself a glass of whatever you have on hand, settle in, and let's begin this easy, enjoyable journey together.

Cheers to you, and to the adventures ahead.

Chapter 1 – Wine Without the Snobbery: The Basics You Need to Know

Wine has a reputation. For some, it brings to mind candlelit dinners, high-end restaurants, and hushed conversations about vintages and rare bottles. For others, it's that intimidating section of the grocery store with rows upon rows of labels in languages they don't understand.

Here's the truth: wine doesn't need to be fancy, complicated, or reserved for special occasions. At its heart, wine is simply fermented grape juice, made to be enjoyed by anyone—whether you're wearing a tuxedo at a wedding or pajamas on your couch.

This chapter is all about breaking wine down to its simplest elements. We'll explore the foundations of wine, talk about different styles and what they mean, and bust a few common myths that might be holding you back. By the end, you'll feel comfortable, confident, and ready to enjoy wine your way.

Wine's Rich History – More Than Just a Fancy Beverage

Wine has been around for thousands of years. Ancient civilizations like the Egyptians, Greeks, and Romans made wine part of their everyday lives. It was used for celebrations, religious ceremonies, and even as medicine.

For much of history, wine wasn't a luxury item. It was a staple, often safer to drink than water and shared among family and friends. Over time, certain regions became known for their exceptional grapes and winemaking traditions. This gave rise to the prestige and mystique that still surround wine today.

Even with its long history, wine has always been about connection. From a rustic Italian vineyard to your neighborhood wine bar, wine is about bringing people together, creating memories, and enhancing life's simple pleasures. That's what we'll focus on here—not complicated rules, but the joy of discovering flavors and experiences you love.

The Three Pillars of Wine Understanding

To truly appreciate wine, it helps to understand three basic concepts. Think of these as the "big picture" ideas that influence everything you taste in your glass. Once you know this, wine becomes far less mysterious.

1. Grapes – The Foundation of Every Wine

At the heart of every wine is the grape. Different grape varieties—or varietals—create very different flavors. Just like apples can taste sweet or tart depending on the type, grapes each have their own unique characteristics.

Here are a few well-known grape varieties:

- **Cabernet Sauvignon** – Bold, rich, and often described as having notes of dark fruit like blackcurrant or blackberry.
- **Pinot Noir** – Lighter and more delicate, with flavors of cherry and soft earthiness.
- **Chardonnay** – Can range from crisp and citrusy to creamy and buttery, depending on how it's made.
- **Riesling** – Typically aromatic and fruity, sometimes sweet and sometimes dry.

Learning to recognize a few common grape varieties is like learning the basics of a new language. You don't need to memorize hundreds of types. Start small, and over time, you'll naturally pick up more.

2. Terroir – The Role of Location

Terroir (pronounced *tare-wahr*) is a fancy French term that simply means "sense of place." It's the combination of soil, climate, and environment where the grapes are grown, and it plays a huge role in how the wine tastes.

Think of terroir like a grape's home. Grapes grown in sunny, warm areas will taste different from those grown in cooler, foggy regions. Even two vineyards just a few miles apart can produce wines with distinct personalities.

For example:

- A Chardonnay grown in California's sunny Napa Valley might taste ripe and tropical.
- The same grape grown in the cooler Burgundy region of France could taste crisper, with notes of green apple and lemon.

Understanding terroir helps explain why wines from different places have such unique characteristics. It's not about memorizing every region, it's about realizing that location matters.

3. The Winemaking Process – From Grape to Glass

The final pillar is how the wine is made. The winemaking process can be as simple or as complex as the winemaker decides. Even small changes during production can completely transform the flavor of the final product.

The basic steps include:

1. **Harvesting** – Grapes are picked when they reach the perfect balance of sugar and acidity.
2. **Crushing and Fermentation** – Grapes are crushed, and yeast begins turning sugar into alcohol.
3. **Aging** – The wine rests in stainless steel tanks, wooden barrels, or a combination of both. This is where flavors develop and deepen.
4. **Bottling** – Once the wine reaches its desired taste, it's bottled and ready to be enjoyed.

Different choices during these steps—like how long to age the wine or what type of barrel to use—create endless variations. This is why two wines made from the same type of grape can taste completely different.

The Main Wine Styles: Red, White, Rosé, and Sparkling

Wine comes in many styles, but nearly every bottle falls into one of four main categories. Knowing the basics will help you navigate a wine list or store shelf with ease.

- **Red Wines**

    Made from dark-skinned grapes, red wines range from light and fruity to bold and intense. Examples: Cabernet Sauvignon, Pinot Noir, Merlot.

- **White Wines**

    Made from green or light-colored grapes, these wines tend to be crisp, bright, and refreshing. Examples: Chardonnay, Sauvignon Blanc, Riesling.

- **Rosé Wines**

    Often called "pink wines," rosé is made by allowing the grape skins to briefly touch the juice, giving it a blush of color. Rosé can be dry or sweet and is perfect for warm weather.

- **Sparkling Wines**

    These wines have bubbles created through natural fermentation or added carbonation. Champagne, Prosecco, and Cava are popular examples, perfect for celebrations or whenever you want a little extra sparkle.

Sweet vs. Dry: Understanding Wine Sweetness

One of the most confusing aspects of wine for beginners is sweetness. People often assume "dry" means bitter, but that's not the case.

- **Dry Wine** – Most of the grape's natural sugar has been converted into alcohol during fermentation. The wine won't taste sugary, even if it has fruity flavors.
- **Off-Dry Wine** – Slightly sweet, with just a touch of sugar remaining.
- **Sweet Wine** – Noticeably sweet, like dessert wines or certain Rieslings.

Understanding this helps you choose wines you'll enjoy. If you like sweeter drinks, start with off-dry or sweet wines. If you prefer less sugar, go for dry options.

How Alcohol Content Shapes the Experience

The alcohol level in wine can affect its body and flavor. Wines with higher alcohol content often feel richer and warmer, while lower-alcohol wines tend to feel lighter and more refreshing.

- **Lower Alcohol (8–11%)** – Light-bodied and easy to sip, like some Rieslings or sparkling wines.
- **Moderate Alcohol (12–14%)** – Most table wines fall into this range, offering balance and versatility.
- **Higher Alcohol (15% or more)** – Bold, full-bodied wines like certain Zinfandels or fortified wines such as Port.

This isn't about getting tipsy—it's about understanding how alcohol interacts with flavor and texture so you can find the styles you enjoy most.

Myth-Busting: Wine Edition

Wine comes with plenty of myths that can discourage beginners. Let's clear up a couple of the most common ones.

Myth #1: Expensive wine is always better.
Price does not guarantee quality. Many affordable wines are delicious, and some high-priced bottles may not suit your personal taste. Trust your palate, not the price tag.

Myth #2: Only experts can pair wines well.
You don't need formal training to match wine with food. A few simple guidelines—and a willingness to experiment—are all you need. Pairing is about enjoyment, not perfection.

Wrapping Up

Wine isn't about memorizing rules or impressing others. It's about discovering flavors, enjoying experiences, and finding what makes *you* smile with each sip.

By understanding these basic concepts, grapes, terroir, and the winemaking process, you've already taken the first step toward becoming a confident wine enthusiast.

In the next chapter, we'll look at the tools you need to make enjoying wine easier and more fun, without cluttering your kitchen or your budget.

Chapter 2 – Essential Wine Gear (Without the Gadget Overload)

Wine culture can sometimes feel like a never-ending catalog of gadgets and tools. Walk into a specialty store or browse online, and you'll find dozens of accessories promising to make your wine taste better, last longer, or look fancier.

Here's the truth: you don't need most of them.

When you're starting out, a few well-chosen essentials will make a huge difference in your wine experience. Everything else is optional. This chapter will help you figure out what's worth having, what's nice to have if you enjoy entertaining, and what you can skip entirely. By the end, you'll know exactly how to equip yourself without cluttering your kitchen—or draining your wallet.

The Bare Essentials: What You Truly Need

When it comes to wine, you can get started with just three key items. These basics will cover nearly every situation, whether you're enjoying a glass on your own or hosting friends.

1. A Reliable Corkscrew

There are countless corkscrew designs out there, but you only need one that works well and feels comfortable to use.

Manual Corkscrews

- Simple and affordable.
- The classic style most people recognize, often called a "waiter's corkscrew."
- Compact and easy to store, perfect for small kitchens or travel.
- With a little practice, it's quick and efficient.

Electric Corkscrews

- Ideal if you struggle with wrist strength or just want extra convenience.
- They open bottles effortlessly at the press of a button.
- Bulkier and require batteries or charging, but they make opening wine almost foolproof.

Tip:
If you're on a budget, start with a manual corkscrew. As your wine hobby grows, you can always upgrade later.

2. Universal Wine Glasses

You might have seen sets of glasses labeled for specific wines—one for red, one for white, another for sparkling, and so on. While these can be fun for serious collectors, they aren't necessary for beginners.

A couple of **universal wine glasses** will work beautifully for almost any wine you pour. Look for glasses that:

- Have a slight bowl shape to allow swirling and aroma release.
- Are comfortable to hold.
- Are sturdy enough for regular use, so you don't have to panic every time you wash them.

Pro Tip:
Clear glass is best, so you can appreciate the color of your wine. Avoid overly decorated or tinted glasses at first.

3. A Stopper or Vacuum Sealer

Unless you always finish a bottle the same day you open it, you'll want a way to keep leftover wine fresh. A simple wine stopper will help prevent spills and limit exposure to air.

For an even better seal, a small vacuum pump with reusable stoppers can help extend the life of an open bottle by removing excess oxygen. These are inexpensive and worth the small investment if you don't drink wine every day.

Nice-to-Have Extras

Once you have the essentials, you might consider adding a couple of tools that can enhance your experience, especially if you enjoy hosting or exploring different wine styles.

Decanter

A decanter is a glass vessel used to gently pour wine out of its bottle before serving. While it might seem like a purely decorative piece, it has a practical purpose.

Why Decant Wine:

- **Aeration:** Exposing wine to air softens harsh flavors and brings out aromas.
- **Sediment Removal:** Some older red wines develop sediment that you don't want in your glass.

You don't need a fancy or expensive decanter—a simple, affordable design works just as well as a high-end one.

When to Use It:

- Young red wines like Cabernet Sauvignon or Syrah/Shiraz often benefit from a bit of aeration.
- Old wines with visible sediment should be decanted slowly and carefully.

Wine Chiller or Bucket

Serving wine at the right temperature makes a big difference in taste. A basic wine chiller or even a small ice bucket can keep whites, rosés, and sparkling wines refreshingly cool during gatherings.

If you don't have one, don't worry. A simple bowl filled with ice water works just as well in a pinch.

Fun Extras

These aren't necessary, but they can add a touch of personality and fun to your wine experience, especially for parties or themed gatherings.

- **Wine Aerators:**
  Small devices that speed up the aeration process by swirling wine as you pour. Helpful, but not essential, especially if you have a decanter.
- **Wine Charms:**
  Colorful markers or charms that help guests keep track of their glasses during parties. They add flair and prevent mix-ups.
- **Decorative Stoppers:**
  A fun way to personalize your wine accessories. Some even feature whimsical designs like animals, flowers, or seasonal themes.

These items are purely for enjoyment, so feel free to add them only if they make you smile.

Avoiding Gadget Overload

It's easy to get caught up in marketing hype. Wine gadgets are everywhere, and many of them promise to "revolutionize" the way you drink. Most of these tools end up collecting dust in a drawer.

Before buying anything new, ask yourself:

- Will this genuinely improve my wine experience?
- Do I already have something that serves the same purpose?
- Is this a need or just a novelty?

Focusing on quality over quantity will save you space, money, and frustration. Remember, wine is meant to be simple and enjoyable—not a hobby that requires a storage unit full of tools.

Easy Storage Solutions for Small Spaces

You don't need a wine cellar or even a dedicated wine fridge to store your bottles properly. A few simple adjustments can keep your wine in good shape until you're ready to enjoy it.

Basic Storage Tips:

- **Avoid Direct Sunlight:** Keep bottles away from windows or bright lights, which can damage wine over time.
- **Stable Temperature:** Store wine in a cool, consistent place. Room temperature is fine, as long as it doesn't fluctuate wildly.
- **Sideways Storage:** If your wine has corks, store bottles on their sides to keep the corks moist and prevent them from drying out.
- **Small Racks:** Affordable countertop or under-cabinet racks are perfect for small collections.

If you only keep a few bottles at a time, even a closet shelf can work perfectly well.

Wrapping Up

Starting your wine journey doesn't mean you need to fill your home with expensive gadgets or specialized equipment. A good corkscrew, a couple of versatile glasses, and a reliable stopper are more than enough to get you started.

From there, you can add extras like a decanter or wine chiller if and when they fit your lifestyle. Remember, the goal is to make wine accessible, not complicated.

In the next chapter, we'll explore how to read a wine bottle label like a pro, so you can walk confidently into any wine shop and know exactly what you're looking at.

Chapter 3 – Wine 101: How to Read a Bottle Like a Pro

Picture this: you're standing in the wine aisle, surrounded by shelves packed with bottles. Some have fancy script lettering, others feature bold modern designs, and a few display names you can't even pronounce.

One label says, "Estate Bottled." Another boasts "Old Vine" and "Reserve."
Some have vintage years listed while others don't.

It can feel like wine producers are speaking a secret language designed to confuse you. And let's be honest, for many beginners, it *is* confusing.

The good news? Once you learn to decode the basics, wine labels become far less intimidating. Instead of guessing, you'll be able to confidently choose a bottle you'll enjoy—whether you're shopping at a local store, picking something for a dinner party, or ordering off a restaurant menu.

This chapter will show you how to read a wine label like a pro, one element at a time.

The Key Parts of a Wine Label

Every wine label, no matter how fancy or simple, provides certain pieces of information. Understanding these core details will help you figure out what you're buying before you pop the cork.

1. Grape Variety

The grape variety—or varietal—is the type of grape used to make the wine. This is often the most helpful clue about what the wine will taste like.

For example:

- **Cabernet Sauvignon:** Bold and rich, with dark fruit flavors like blackcurrant or blackberry.
- **Pinot Noir:** Lighter and more delicate, often featuring cherry and earthy notes.
- **Chardonnay:** Can range from crisp and citrusy to creamy and buttery, depending on how it's made.
- **Riesling:** Fragrant and versatile, ranging from bone-dry to sweet.

In countries like the United States and Australia, the grape variety is almost always listed prominently on the label. This makes it easier for beginners to match wines to their personal taste.

Note: In some European countries, especially France and Italy, the grape variety may not be listed at all. Instead, the label will show the region, and you'll need to know which grapes are typically grown there. Don't worry, we'll cover this shortly.

2. Region

The region tells you where the grapes were grown. This matters because climate, soil, and local winemaking traditions all influence the final flavor, a concept known as **terroir**.

Some regions are large, covering entire states or countries, while others are very specific, referring to small towns or even single vineyards.

Examples:

- **California** – A broad region, meaning grapes could come from anywhere within the state.
- **Napa Valley** – A much smaller, prestigious area within California known for high-quality wines.
- **Bordeaux (France)** – Indicates a wine made in Bordeaux, which has strict rules about grape types and winemaking practices.

Knowing a bit about regions can help you predict the style and quality of a wine. Generally, the more specific the region listed, the more distinctive the wine's flavor profile will be.

3. Vintage Year

The vintage year is the year the grapes were harvested. It can give you insight into the wine's character and readiness to drink.

- **Vintage Wine:** Made entirely from grapes harvested in a single year.
- **Non-Vintage Wine:** A blend of grapes from multiple years, often found in sparkling wines like Champagne.

Weather conditions during a particular year can affect the flavor and quality of the wine. Some vintages produce exceptional wines, while others may be less remarkable.

For most everyday wines, you don't need to stress over the vintage year, but it's helpful to note if you plan to keep a bottle for a special occasion or compare different harvests of the same wine.

4. Alcohol Content

The alcohol content, measured as **ABV (Alcohol by Volume)**, can influence both flavor and body.

- **Lower Alcohol (8–11%)** – Light-bodied, crisp, and refreshing. Examples include many Rieslings or sparkling wines.
- **Moderate Alcohol (12–14%)** – Most table wines fall here, offering balance and versatility.
- **Higher Alcohol (15% or more)** – Bold, full-bodied wines like certain Zinfandels or fortified wines.

A higher alcohol level often means a richer mouthfeel, while lower alcohol wines tend to be lighter and more refreshing. This detail can help you choose a wine that suits the mood or meal.

Common Wine Terms Made Simple

Wine labels often include words that sound impressive but don't always make sense to beginners. Here's what some of the most common ones mean:

- **Reserve:**
  Traditionally, "Reserve" indicated a higher-quality wine aged longer before release. Today, the term isn't legally regulated in many countries, so it can simply be a marketing term. Some wineries use it sincerely, others don't.
- **Old Vine (Vieilles Vignes in French):**
  Refers to wines made from older grapevines, which usually produce smaller, more concentrated grapes. These wines can be more complex, though "old" can mean different ages depending on the region.
- **Estate Bottled:**
  This means the winery grew the grapes, produced the wine, and bottled it on-site. It suggests greater control over the process and can indicate higher quality.
- **Single Vineyard:**
  All the grapes came from one specific vineyard. These wines often showcase the unique characteristics of that location.

Understanding these terms helps you avoid being swayed by fancy words alone.

International Wine Labeling Differences

Not all countries label their wines the same way. Here's a simple breakdown of how major wine-producing regions differ:

United States

- Typically, straightforward and beginner friendly.
- The grape variety is usually front and center, such as "Cabernet Sauvignon" or "Chardonnay."
- The region (like California or Oregon) is clearly marked.
- Alcohol content and vintage year are always included.

Example:

"2019 Napa Valley Cabernet Sauvignon"

France

- Labels focus on the region rather than the grape variety.
- Certain regions are strongly associated with specific grapes, so locals don't need them spelled out.

Examples:

- **Bordeaux:** Usually a blend of Cabernet Sauvignon, Merlot, and other grapes.
- **Burgundy (Bourgogne):** Primarily Pinot Noir for reds and Chardonnay for whites.
- **Champagne:** Always sparkling wine, made under strict rules.

French labels can seem intimidating, but once you learn the key regions, they become much easier to navigate.

Italy

- Similar to France, with emphasis on regions and appellations (controlled designations of origin).
- Well-known examples:
    - **Chianti:** Typically made from Sangiovese grapes.
    - **Barolo:** A bold red made from Nebbiolo grapes.
    - **Prosecco:** A popular sparkling wine.

Italian wines may also include terms like **DOC** or **DOCG**, which indicate quality levels set by Italian law.

Australia

- Like the U.S., Australian labels are clear and straightforward.
- The grape variety and region are both clearly listed, making them easy for beginners to read.

Example:

"2021 Barossa Valley Shiraz"

How to Spot Value Wines

Not every great wine has a high price tag. In fact, some of the best bottles are surprisingly affordable once you know what to look for.

Tips for finding hidden gems:

1. **Look Beyond the Big Names:**
   Lesser-known regions often produce excellent wines at lower prices.
2. **Ask for Recommendations:**
   Don't be afraid to ask store staff or restaurant servers for their favorites under a certain budget.
3. **Try Different Vintages:**
   A previous year's wine might be discounted to make room for new stock, and it's often just as good.
4. **Experiment with Blends:**
   Blended wines can be both delicious and budget friendly.

By combining these strategies, you can drink well without spending a fortune.

Mini-Exercise: Comparing Two Labels

Here's a fun way to put your new knowledge to use. The next time you're at a wine shop, grab two bottles and compare their labels side by side. Look for:

- The grape variety
- The region
- The vintage year
- Any extra terms like "Reserve" or "Estate Bottled"
- The alcohol content

Notice how much information you can gather before even tasting the wine.

This simple exercise will build your confidence and help you make informed choices every time you shop.

Wrapping Up

Wine labels might seem like a puzzle at first, but now you have the keys to solve it. By understanding the basic parts—grape variety, region, vintage year, and alcohol content—you can walk into any store and feel empowered, not overwhelmed.

In the next chapter, we'll dive deeper into the world of wine styles, exploring the differences between reds, whites, rosés, and sparkling wines so you can start recognizing your personal favorites.

Chapter 4 – Reds, Whites, and Rosés: The Big Categories

When you walk through the wine aisle, you'll notice that every bottle falls into one of a few main categories: red, white, rosé, or sparkling. Each category has its own personality, flavor profiles, and ideal occasions.

Understanding these broad groups will help you feel more confident choosing wines you'll enjoy. By the end of this chapter, you'll have a mental "map" of wine styles and a solid starting point for exploring more specific varieties later on.

Red Wines: Bold, Smooth, and Everything In Between

Red wines are made from dark-skinned grapes. During the winemaking process, the juice stays in contact with the grape skins, which adds color, tannins (natural compounds that affect texture and structure), and deeper flavors.

Red wines can range from light and silky to rich and powerful. Here are a few popular reds you'll likely encounter, explained in everyday terms.

Cabernet Sauvignon – The Classic Heavyweight

Cabernet Sauvignon is one of the most widely recognized red wines in the world. It's bold, structured, and full of rich flavors.

Flavor Profile:

Think of dark fruits like blackcurrant, blackberry, and plum, with hints of spice, tobacco, or even a touch of vanilla if aged in oak barrels.

Body:

Full-bodied, meaning it feels heavier and more robust in your mouth.

Occasions:

Perfect for hearty meals like steak, roast lamb, or a juicy burger. Cabernet Sauvignon shines at dinner parties or special celebrations.

Pinot Noir – Light, Elegant, and Easy-Drinking

Pinot Noir is often described as the "romantic" red. It's lighter and more delicate than Cabernet Sauvignon, making it approachable for beginners.

Flavor Profile:
Bright red fruits like cherry, raspberry, or strawberry, with subtle earthy undertones. Sometimes you'll notice a hint of mushroom or forest floor—that's normal and adds complexity.

Body:
Light to medium-bodied, smooth, and silky.

Occasions:
A versatile wine that pairs well with poultry, salmon, or vegetarian dishes. Great for casual dinners or cozy nights in.

Merlot – Smooth and Crowd-Pleasing

Merlot has a reputation for being soft, approachable, and universally liked. It's an excellent choice for someone just starting to explore red wine.

Flavor Profile:

Plummy and velvety, with notes of cherry, blackberry, and chocolate. Some Merlots are slightly spicy, while others lean more toward smooth fruitiness.

Body:

Medium-bodied, with a round, easy-drinking texture.

Occasions:

Ideal for gatherings where you need a wine everyone will enjoy. It is paired well with pasta, pizza, and roasted chicken.

Syrah/Shiraz – Bold and Spicy

Syrah and Shiraz are two names for the same grape, with "Syrah" often used in France and "Shiraz" in Australia. The style can vary depending on where it's grown, but it's known for bold, intense flavors.

Flavor Profile:
Dark fruit flavors like blackberry and blueberry, with peppery spice and smoky undertones. Some versions may even have hints of cured meat or herbs.

Body:
Medium to full-bodied, with lots of personality.

Occasions:
Perfect for barbecue nights, grilled meats, or dishes with strong flavors like spicy sausages.

White Wines: Crisp, Buttery, or Floral

White wines are typically made from green or light-skinned grapes. The juice is separated from the skins early in the process, resulting in a lighter color and different flavor profile.

White wines are incredibly versatile, ranging from zesty and refreshing to smooth and creamy. Here are some of the most popular varieties you'll encounter.

Chardonnay – The Chameleon of White Wines

Chardonnay can taste completely different depending on how it's made, which is why it's often called the "chameleon" of white wines.

Flavor Profile:

- **Unoaked Chardonnay:** Crisp and refreshing, with flavors of green apple, lemon, and pear.
- **Oaked Chardonnay:** Creamier, with notes of butter, vanilla, and toasted nuts.

Body:
Ranges from light and crisp to rich and full-bodied.

Occasions:
Pairs beautifully with poultry, seafood, or creamy pasta dishes. A crowd-pleasing wine that works well for both casual and formal meals.

Sauvignon Blanc – Bright and Zesty

Sauvignon Blanc is known for its crisp acidity and vibrant flavors. It's a refreshing choice, especially in warm weather.

Flavor Profile:
Citrus fruits like lime and grapefruit, with herbal or grassy notes. In some regions, you might notice tropical hints like passion fruit or pineapple.

Body:
Light-bodied and lively.

Occasions:
Perfect for salads, light appetizers, and outdoor picnics. A go-to wine for summer evenings.

Riesling – Sweet or Dry, Always Aromatic

Riesling is one of the most versatile white wines. It can be made in a range of styles, from bone-dry to lusciously sweet.

Flavor Profile:

Fruity and aromatic, with flavors of peach, apricot, and honey. Even dry Rieslings have a distinctive floral quality and bright acidity.

Body:

Light-bodied and highly refreshing.

Occasions:

Excellent with spicy foods like Thai or Indian cuisine, as its sweetness balances heat beautifully.

Pinot Grigio – Light and Refreshing

Pinot Grigio (called Pinot Gris in France) is a reliable choice for those who like a clean, straightforward wine.

Flavor Profile:

Delicate flavors of citrus, green apple, and pear. It's simple, crisp, and easy to drink.

Body:

Light-bodied, with a smooth finish.

Occasions:

Great for casual sipping, seafood dishes, or light appetizers.

Rosé: More Than Just "Pink Wine"

Rosé often gets dismissed as just a summertime trend or a sweet, sugary drink. In reality, rosé can be incredibly diverse and complex, bridging the gap between red and white wines.

How It's Made:
Rosé gets its color by allowing the grape skins to briefly touch the juice—long enough to create that blush hue, but not long enough to make it a red wine.

Dry vs. Sweet Rosés

- **Dry Rosé:** Crisp, refreshing, and not sugary. These wines pair well with a variety of foods and are popular in regions like Provence, France.
- **Sweet Rosé:** Slightly or noticeably sweet, making it approachable for beginners who enjoy sweeter drinks. Examples include White Zinfandel.

Rosé is incredibly versatile. It works just as well at a summer picnic as it does at a fancy brunch or casual weeknight dinner.

Sparkling Wines: A Touch of Celebration

Sparkling wine is perfect for special occasions, but it's also delightful on an ordinary day when you want to add a little sparkle. The bubbles are created through natural fermentation or, in some cases, added carbonation.

Popular Types of Sparkling Wine

- **Champagne:** Produced exclusively in the Champagne region of France under strict guidelines. Known for its elegance and complexity.
- **Prosecco:** An Italian sparkling wine that's typically lighter, fruitier, and more affordable.
- **Cava:** A Spanish sparkling wine that offers great quality at a reasonable price.

Sweetness Levels: Brut, Extra Dry, Demi-Sec

Sparkling wine labels often include terms that indicate sweetness. Here's what they mean:

- **Brut:** Very dry, with little to no sweetness.
- **Extra Dry:** Slightly sweeter than Brut, despite the name.
- **Demi-Sec:** Noticeably sweet, perfect for desserts or those who prefer sweeter wines.

Understanding these terms helps you choose a sparkling wine that matches your taste and the occasion.

Quick Reference Cheat Sheet

Here's a simple snapshot of the wines we've discussed so far:

Category	Examples	Flavor Profile	Body	Best Occasions
Red	Cabernet Sauvignon, Pinot Noir, Merlot, Syrah/Shiraz	Dark fruit, spice, earthy, bold or smooth	Light to Full	Dinner parties, hearty meals
White	Chardonnay, Sauvignon Blanc, Riesling, Pinot Grigio	Citrus, floral, buttery, crisp	Light to Full	Casual dinners, seafood, summer sipping
Rosé	Provence Rosé, White Zinfandel	Dry and crisp or lightly sweet	Light	Picnics, brunch, casual gatherings
Sparkling	Champagne, Prosecco, Cava	Fruity, crisp, bubbly	Light	Celebrations, special toasts, appetizers

Wrapping Up

By now, you've been introduced to the four main wine categories and several popular varieties within each one. You've also learned how body, flavor, and sweetness affect the overall experience.

With this foundation, you'll start to develop a sense of which wines you naturally gravitate toward. In the next chapter, we'll take things a step further by learning how to taste wine like a pro—without any of the pretentiousness or pressure.

Chapter 5 – How to Taste Wine (Without Feeling Silly)

Wine tasting can feel intimidating if you've only seen it done in movies or at formal events. You know the scene: someone holds their glass up to the light, swirls it dramatically, takes a slow sip, and then starts talking about "notes of leather, dark cherry, and freshly turned earth."

It can make you wonder, *"Am I supposed to taste all that? And what if all I notice is... well, grapes?"*

The truth is that wine tasting isn't about proving your skills or impressing anyone. It's about slowing down and truly experiencing what's in your glass. Anyone can do it—and you don't need a fancy vocabulary or years of practice to start.

In this chapter, you'll learn the simple, five-step process for tasting wine with confidence. By the end, you'll not only know how to evaluate a wine, but you'll also understand what you personally enjoy. And best of all, you'll realize there's no "wrong" way to taste wine.

The 5 S's of Wine Tasting

To keep things simple, wine tasting can be broken down into five easy steps known as the **5 S's**: See, Swirl, Smell, Sip, and Savor. Think of this as a guided exploration rather than a rigid rulebook. These steps help you slow down, pay attention, and get the most out of each glass.

1. See – Observe the Wine

Start by simply looking at the wine in your glass. Hold it up to the light or against a white background, like a napkin or piece of paper.

What to Notice:

- **Color and Depth:** Reds may range from pale ruby to deep, almost purple hues. Whites can vary from nearly clear to golden yellow. Rosés will show shades of pink, peach, or salmon.
- **Clarity:** Is the wine clear and bright, or cloudy and hazy? Most wines are clear, but natural or unfiltered wines may look slightly cloudy.
- **Age Clues:** Generally, red wines become lighter around the edges as they age, while white wines deepen in color over time.

This step is quick, but it helps set the stage for the rest of your tasting.

2. Swirl – Release the Aromas

Next, gently swirl the wine in your glass. This might feel awkward at first, but you don't need to be dramatic. A slow, small circular motion is all it takes.

Why Swirl?

Swirling introduces air to the wine, which releases aromas and opens up its flavors. Think of it like waking the wine up after a long nap.

Tip for Beginners:

If you're nervous about spilling, keep the base of your glass on the table while you swirl. It's safer and just as effective.

3. Smell – Take in the Aromas

Your sense of smell plays a huge role in how you experience wine. After swirling, bring the glass to your nose and take a slow, deep sniff. Don't rush, this is where the fun begins.

Things to Consider:

- Do you smell fruit? If so, what kind—berries, citrus, stone fruit, tropical fruit?
- Are there earthy or herbal scents, like fresh soil, mushrooms, or herbs?
- Do you notice spices, vanilla, or toasty notes from oak aging?

Don't overthink it. There's no right or wrong answer. Everyone's nose is different, and what you smell might not match what someone else detects.

If all you smell is "wine," that's okay too. Over time, your ability to pick out specific aromas will improve naturally.

4. Sip – Taste the Wine

Now comes the best part: tasting. Take a small sip and let the wine spread across your tongue. Hold it there for a moment before swallowing or spitting (spitting is common at professional tastings, but completely optional at home).

What to Notice:

- **Flavor:** Identify the main flavors. Is it fruity, earthy, spicy, or floral?
- **Texture:** Does it feel light and crisp, smooth and silky, or bold and mouth-filling?
- **Balance:** Do the flavors work well together, or does one element overpower the others?

Some people take a small breath of air while the wine is in their mouth to enhance the flavors, but don't feel pressured to do this right away. Focus on simply noticing what you like or don't like.

5. Savor – Reflect on the Experience

The final step is to pause and think about what you just tasted. This helps you remember what you enjoyed and builds confidence for future tastings.

Ask yourself:

- Did I like this wine?
- What stood out most—flavor, texture, aroma?
- Would I choose it again or try something similar?

Wine tasting is as much about self-discovery as it is about the wine itself. The more you practice, the clearer your preferences will become.

Describing What You Taste (Without Sounding Pretentious)

One of the most intimidating parts of wine tasting is describing the flavors. The key is to keep it simple. Use everyday words instead of fancy terminology.

Common Descriptors:

- **Fruity:** Notes of berry, citrus, apple, or tropical fruit.
- **Earthy:** Mushroom, soil, wet leaves, or mineral-like flavors.
- **Spicy:** Pepper, cinnamon, clove, or baking spices.
- **Floral:** Honeysuckle, rose, jasmine, or other delicate aromas.

For example, instead of saying, *"This wine has pronounced aromas of cassis and forest floor,"* you could simply say, *"It tastes like dark berries with a touch of earthiness."*

The goal is to express what *you* experience, not to sound like a textbook.

Why "Legs" Don't Really Matter

You've probably seen people swirl a glass of wine and then point out the streaks of liquid that run down the inside. These are called "legs" or "tears."

Contrary to popular belief, legs don't indicate quality. They simply show the wine's alcohol and sugar content. A wine with higher alcohol or sugar will have thicker, slower-moving legs.

While they can be interesting to observe, they aren't a reliable way to judge whether a wine is "good." Consider them a fun visual, nothing more.

Fun Tasting Game: Blind Wine Challenge

Tasting wine doesn't have to be serious. In fact, making it playful can take the pressure off and help you learn even faster.

Here's how to host a blind tasting game:

1. Gather a few friends and pick three to five different wines.
2. Slip each bottle into a plain brown paper bag so the labels are hidden.
3. Pour small samples into each person's glass, one wine at a time.
4. Taste together and take turns describing what you notice.
5. After everyone has guessed, reveal the wines and compare impressions.

This activity is a great way to see how personal taste varies. You'll be surprised at how much fun it is to discover favorites without being influenced by labels or prices.

Optional Tasting Notes (No Printables Required)

While we won't include printable sheets in this book, you can easily jot down notes in a small notebook or on your phone.

When tasting, consider writing down:

- The wine's name and type
- Flavors or aromas you noticed
- Whether you liked it and why
- What food you paired it with

Over time, these notes become a personalized guide to your preferences, helping you remember which wines you loved—and which you didn't.

Wrapping Up

Wine tasting doesn't need to feel intimidating or overly formal. By following the **5 S's—See, Swirl, Smell, Sip, and Savor—you can confidently explore the world of wine** while having fun along the way.

Remember, there are no wrong answers when it comes to what you like. The more you taste, the more you'll understand your own preferences.

In the next chapter, we'll take what you've learned about tasting and apply it to food pairing, so you can create simple, delicious matches that make both the wine and the meal shine.

Chapter 6 – Pairing Wine with Food (Simple Rules That Work)

There's something magical about the way wine and food can enhance each other. The right pairing can make a simple meal feel special, turning a Tuesday night dinner into an experience.

But here's the thing: wine pairing doesn't have to be complicated. You don't need to memorize dozens of pairing charts or stress over whether your wine "goes" with the dish you're serving.

The truth is, pairing wine with food is about balance, experimentation, and, most importantly, enjoying yourself. In this chapter, you'll learn a few easy rules, classic pairings that never fail, and fun ideas for trying your own combinations at home.

The Basic Pairing Principle: Match Intensity

If you remember just one guideline, let it be this: **match the intensity of the wine with the intensity of the food.**

Think of wine like another ingredient in your meal. Just as you wouldn't overpower a delicate salad with a rich, heavy sauce, you don't want to drown out a subtle dish with a bold, high-alcohol wine.

Here's what that looks like:

- **Light Foods + Light Wines**
  A crisp Sauvignon Blanc with a fresh garden salad or grilled white fish.
- **Medium Foods + Medium Wines**
  A smooth Merlot with roasted chicken or pasta in a tomato-based sauce.
- **Bold Foods + Bold Wines**
  A robust Cabernet Sauvignon with a juicy steak or lamb chops.

This simple approach works for almost every pairing situation. It keeps your food and wine in harmony rather than letting one overpower the other.

Classic Pairings You'll Hear About

Certain pairings have stood the test of time because they just work. These classics are great starting points if you're feeling unsure.

- **Red Wine with Red Meat**
  Rich red meats like steak, burgers, and roast beef complement bold, tannic red wines like Cabernet Sauvignon or Syrah. The protein and fat in the meat balance the structure of the wine beautifully.
- **White Wine with Fish and Chicken**
  Light, delicate dishes like grilled fish or roasted chicken pair well with crisp whites such as Sauvignon Blanc or Pinot Grigio.
- **Sparkling Wine with Salty Snacks**
  The bubbles and acidity in sparkling wine make it perfect for salty treats like popcorn, chips, or cheese. It's an unexpected but delightful combo.
- **Sweet Wine with Spicy Food**
  A slightly sweet Riesling or Moscato can cool the heat of spicy dishes like Thai curries or Mexican cuisine.

These pairings are classics for a reason, but they're also just a jumping-off point.

Why Rules Are Meant to Be Broken

While pairing guidelines are helpful, they aren't set in stone. Your personal taste matters most.

If you love Chardonnay with steak or Cabernet with seafood, go for it! The best wine is the one *you* enjoy drinking. Experimenting is half the fun, and you may stumble across a unique pairing that surprises you.

Tip:

If you're hosting a dinner and worried about getting it wrong, offer two wine options—a red and a white. Guests can decide which they prefer, and you take the pressure off yourself completely.

Easy Pairing Table for Everyday Foods

Wine pairing isn't just for fancy dinners. It can make everyday meals more fun and flavorful. Here's a simple guide for common foods you might already be cooking or ordering.

Food	Suggested Wine Style	Why It Works
Pizza	Medium-bodied red like Merlot or Chianti	Tomato sauce pairs well with fruity reds.
Burgers	Bold red like Cabernet Sauvignon or Syrah	Matches the richness of the meat and toppings.
Pasta	Light red (Pinot Noir) or white (Chardonnay)	Versatile for creamy or tomato-based sauces.
Cheese	Sparkling wine or crisp white like Sauvignon Blanc	Bubbles and acidity cut through the richness.
Tacos	Slightly sweet Riesling or Rosé	Balances spice and complements fresh toppings.
Grilled Vegetables	Pinot Grigio or light Rosé	Refreshing and enhances the natural flavors.

This table isn't meant to limit you, it's simply a handy starting point for quick decisions.

Fun DIY Wine and Cheese Night

Wine and cheese are a classic duo, and hosting a tasting night with friends is both fun and educational. It doesn't need to be complicated or expensive. Here's how to do it step by step.

Step 1: Choose 3–4 Wines

- Include a mix of styles: one red, one white, one rosé or sparkling.
- Don't worry about price—affordable wines are perfect for a casual tasting.

Step 2: Select 4–5 Cheeses

Aim for a variety of textures and flavors:

- **Soft:** Brie or goat cheese
- **Semi-soft:** Havarti or Fontina
- **Hard:** Cheddar or Parmesan
- **Blue:** Gorgonzola or Roquefort (optional for adventurous palates)

Step 3: Add Some Extras

Round out your spread with simple snacks:

- Crackers or slices of baguette
- Grapes, apple slices, or dried fruits
- Nuts like almonds or walnuts
- A drizzle of honey for contrast

Step 4: Taste and Experiment

Encourage everyone to try different combinations and share their thoughts.

There's no right or wrong here—it's about discovering what each person enjoys most.

Pro Tip:

Label the wines and cheeses so guests can remember their favorites later.

Tips for Hosting Without Stress

If you're planning a wine-focused gathering, keep it simple. The goal is to have fun, not to impress anyone with elaborate presentations.

- **Prep Ahead:**
  Chill white wines and sparkling wines ahead of time and set reds out about 30 minutes before serving to let them breathe.
- **Use What You Have:**
  No need for matching glasses or special serving trays. Everyday dishes work perfectly.
- **Keep Food Simple:**
  Cheese boards, appetizers, and finger foods are easy and crowd-pleasing.
- **Encourage Curiosity:**
  Let guests taste freely and share opinions without pressure. A relaxed atmosphere makes for the best memories.

Wrapping Up

Wine and food pairing doesn't need to be a science experiment or a test of knowledge. It's about creating balance, having fun, and enhancing the experience of eating and drinking together.

By following the simple rule of matching intensity, trying classic pairings, and experimenting with your own combinations, you'll quickly gain confidence.

In the next chapter, we'll focus on buying wine—how to navigate stores, online shops, and restaurants to find delicious bottles without overspending.

Chapter 7 – Buying Wine Without Breaking the Bank

Shopping for wine can feel a little like treasure hunting. There are countless bottles out there, ranging from just a few dollars to hundreds—or even thousands—per bottle. But here's a little secret: great wine doesn't have to come with a hefty price tag.

Whether you're grabbing a bottle for a casual dinner, stocking up for a party, or looking for something a little special, you can absolutely find wines you love without overspending. This chapter will guide you through the ins and outs of wine shopping, showing you how to make smart choices and get the best value for your money.

Understanding Price Tiers

Wine prices can vary dramatically, and sometimes it's hard to tell why one bottle costs $10 while another costs $50 or more. Understanding general price tiers will help you navigate your options with confidence.

Budget Wines ($5–$15 per bottle)

- Widely available at grocery stores, warehouse clubs, and discount retailers.
- These wines are often mass-produced, which helps keep costs low.
- Quality can vary, but there are plenty of reliable, tasty options in this range.
- Perfect for casual weeknight dinners, cooking, or stocking up for larger gatherings.

Tip: Stick with reputable brands or popular varietals like Pinot Grigio, Sauvignon Blanc, Merlot, or Cabernet Sauvignon when shopping in this range.

Mid-Range Wines ($15–$30 per bottle)

- Offers a step up in complexity and craftsmanship.
- You'll find smaller production wines and bottles from well-known wine regions like Napa Valley or Bordeaux.
- This price range often provides the best balance between quality and value.
- Ideal for dinner parties, gifts, or something a little more special when you want.

Premium Wines ($30 and up)

- Often from prestigious vineyards with limited production.
- These wines can age beautifully and may be collectible for enthusiasts.
- While many are excellent, high prices don't always guarantee you'll love the taste.

Important Reminder:

You don't need to spend more than you're comfortable with. A $12 bottle can be just as enjoyable as a $40 one if it suits your preferences and the occasion.

Finding Hidden Gems at Grocery Stores and Local Shops

Grocery stores and local wine shops are treasure troves if you know how to shop smart. Here's how to find those hidden gems:

At Grocery Stores

- **Look Beyond Eye-Level Shelves:**
  Premium brands often pay for prime shelf space. The best deals are sometimes found on the top or bottom rows.

- **Check for Sales and Promotions:**
  Many stores rotate discounts weekly or monthly.

- **Stick with Familiar Grapes:**
  If you're trying a new brand, start with varietals you already enjoy.

At Local Wine Shops

Independent wine shops can be goldmines for unique, high-quality wines at reasonable prices. The staff is often knowledgeable and passionate about wine, which works to your advantage.

- **Build a Relationship:**
  Visit regularly, ask questions, and let them know what you like. Over time, they'll recommend wines tailored to your taste and budget.
- **Be Honest About Price:**
  There's no shame in saying, "I'm looking for a great bottle under $15."
  Good shops are happy to help you find value without upselling.
- **Ask About Lesser-Known Regions:**
  Wines from emerging areas often offer better prices than big-name regions.

The Importance of Asking Staff for Recommendations

Whether you're at a grocery store or specialty shop, don't be afraid to ask for help. Most employees love sharing their knowledge and guiding customers toward great finds.

When asking for recommendations:

- Mention the type of wine you like (for example, "I enjoy crisp, refreshing whites" or "I like bold reds with a little spice").
- Share what you're eating, if it's for a specific meal.
- Be upfront about your budget.

You'll be surprised at how often you'll walk away with a fantastic bottle you might not have chosen on your own.

How to Buy Wine Online Safely

Buying wine online has become incredibly popular, especially with so many options and delivery services available. However, it's important to shop carefully to avoid disappointment—or worse, counterfeit bottles.

Tips for safe online wine shopping:

1. **Choose Trusted Retailers:**
   Stick with reputable online stores or directly from winery websites.
2. **Check Shipping Laws:**
   Wine shipping rules vary by state. Make sure the seller can legally ship to your area.
3. **Read Descriptions Carefully:**
   Look for details like vintage, region, and tasting notes to ensure you're getting what you expect.
4. **Watch for Shipping Costs:**
   Some sites offer free shipping with minimum purchases—take advantage of these deals when possible.

Navigating Wine Club Memberships

Wine clubs can be a fun way to try new wines regularly, but they aren't all created equal. Some are excellent, while others may not be worth the cost.

Questions to ask before joining:

- How often will you receive shipments, and how many bottles per shipment?
- Can you customize your selections, or are they pre-chosen?
- What is the total cost, including shipping and taxes?
- Are there perks, like discounts on additional purchases?

Pro Tip:
Start with a short-term membership or trial before committing long-term. This way, you can see if the club matches your taste and budget.

Understanding "House Wines" at Restaurants

Many restaurants offer a "house wine," often listed simply as red or white. While house wines can vary widely in quality, they're usually chosen because they're versatile, affordable, and pair well with a variety of dishes.

- **Ask Questions:** Don't be shy about asking what the house wine is and where it's from.
- **Consider Value:** House wines are usually priced lower than other options, making them a good choice for casual dining.
- **Upgrade When Needed:** If you're celebrating a special occasion, it may be worth exploring the next tier up on the wine list.

Fun Challenge: Three Wines Under $15

Here's a playful way to expand your wine knowledge without spending a fortune. Next time you shop, pick up three different bottles, each under $15. Try to choose:

1. A red wine
2. A white wine
3. A wild card (rosé, sparkling, or a varietal you've never tried)

How to do the challenge:

- Taste each wine over the course of a week, taking notes about what you like and dislike.
- Compare them side by side, if possible, and notice how they differ.
- Decide which one you'd buy again and why.

This challenge builds your palate and helps you discover new favorites—while keeping things budget-friendly.

Wrapping Up

Wine shopping doesn't have to be intimidating or expensive. With a little knowledge and a willingness to ask questions, you can find delicious wines at any price point.

Whether you're exploring grocery store deals, supporting a local wine shop, or shopping online, the key is to focus on what you enjoy—not what costs the most or looks the fanciest.

In the next chapter, we'll explore how to store and serve wine, so it stays fresh and tastes its best, even if you don't have a fancy wine cellar or expensive equipment.

Chapter 8 – Storing and Serving Wine the Easy Way

Imagine this: you bring home a bottle of wine you're excited to try, open it for a special evening, and the first sip is… disappointing. It tastes flat, sour, or just "off."

Often, this isn't the wine's fault, it's how it was stored or served. Proper storage and serving techniques can make a huge difference to your wine experience. The good news? You don't need a fancy wine cellar, high-end gadgets, or a lot of space to get it right.

In this chapter, we'll cover easy ways to keep your wine fresh, the ideal serving temperatures for different styles, how to rescue a wine that's starting to fade, and what to do with leftovers. With just a few simple steps, you'll make every glass taste its best.

Ideal Wine Storage Conditions

Wine is sensitive to its surroundings. Light, temperature, and humidity all play a role in how it ages and how it tastes when you finally pour a glass. Think of wine like a delicate ingredient—it needs to be handled with care.

1. Light

Direct sunlight or bright artificial light can damage wine over time. The UV rays essentially "cook" the wine, causing unpleasant flavors.

Quick Fix:

- Store wine in a dark cabinet, pantry, or closet.
- If you keep wine on open shelves, choose a spot away from windows or use a curtain or door to block light.

2. Temperature

Fluctuating temperatures are wine's worst enemy. When wine gets too warm or too cold, it can expand and contract inside the bottle, damaging the flavor and even loosening the cork.

Ideal Temperature Range:

- **45–65°F (7–18°C)** is perfect for most wines.
- A consistent, cool spot is more important than hitting the exact number.

Tip for Apartment Living:

If you don't have a wine fridge, aim for the coolest part of your home, such as a low cabinet or closet floor. Avoid areas near ovens, radiators, or heat vents.

3. Humidity

Humidity matters mainly for wines with cork closures. If the cork dries out, air can seep in and spoil the wine.

Easy Solution:

- A little moisture in the air helps, but you don't need to obsess over it.
- In very dry climates, storing corked bottles on their sides helps keep the cork moist.

Quick Tips for Those Without a Wine Cellar

Not everyone has space—or budget—for a dedicated wine cellar. Luckily, most people don't need one. These simple strategies will keep your wine in great shape:

- **Pantry or Closet Storage:** A dark, cool area is perfect for short- to medium-term storage.
- **Small Wine Rack:** Keeps bottles organized and stored sideways.
- **Avoid the Kitchen Counter:** Kitchens get warm and bright, which isn't ideal for wine.
- **Fridge for Short-Term Needs:** If you plan to drink a bottle within a few days, your regular refrigerator works just fine.

Remember, wine doesn't need to be treated like a fragile museum piece. A little care goes a long way.

Serving Temperature Guide

Serving wine at the right temperature brings out its best flavors. Too warm, and wine can taste dull or overly alcoholic. Too cold, and the aromas and flavors may be muted.

Here's a simple guide you can rely on:

Wine Type	Ideal Serving Temperature	Quick Tips
Sparkling Wine	40–50°F (4–10°C)	Chill in the fridge for 3 hours or in an ice bucket for 30 minutes before serving.
White Wine	45–55°F (7–13°C)	Chill for 2 hours in the fridge, then let it sit out for 10 minutes before pouring.
Rosé Wine	45–55°F (7–13°C)	Same as white wine—cool, but not icy.
Red Wine	55–65°F (13–18°C)	If your home is warm, chill the bottle for 20–30 minutes before serving.

Pro Tip:

"Room temperature" for red wine traditionally referred to cool European cellars—not modern, heated homes. If a red wine feels too warm, don't be afraid to give it a quick chill.

How to Revive an "Off" Bottle

Sometimes you open a bottle, and the first sip seems a little flat or unbalanced. Before giving up, try these simple fixes:

1. **Let It Breathe:**
   Pour the wine into a decanter or even just a wide glass. Give it 15–30 minutes to interact with the air. This can help soften harsh flavors and bring out hidden aromas.
2. **Chill It Slightly:**
   If a wine tastes sharp or too alcoholic, a quick 10-minute chill in the fridge can smooth things out.
3. **Add Food:**
   Some wines taste better when paired with food. A cheese plate or savory snack can change how the wine comes across.

If none of these tricks help, the wine may truly be past its prime—but at least you gave it a fair chance.

How Long Wine Lasts After Opening

Once a bottle is opened, oxygen begins to interact with the wine, gradually changing its flavor. Here's how long you can expect different wines to stay fresh with proper storage:

- **Sparkling Wine:** 1–2 days with a sparkling wine stopper.
- **White and Rosé Wines:** 3–5 days in the fridge with a regular stopper or vacuum seal.
- **Red Wines:** 3–5 days, stored in a cool, dark spot with the cork or stopper firmly in place.
- **Fortified Wines (like Port):** Up to a month, thanks to their higher alcohol content.

Tip:
If you know you won't finish a bottle, consider pouring half into a smaller container right after opening. Less air in the container means slower oxidation.

Storing Leftover Wine for Cooking

Even if a wine isn't ideal for sipping anymore, it can still be perfect for cooking. A splash of wine can transform sauces, stews, and even desserts.

How to Save It:

- **Refrigerate:** Keep the leftover wine in the fridge with a tight seal.
- **Use Within 1–2 Weeks:** While it won't taste great to drink, it will still add flavor to your recipes.
- **Freeze in Portions:** Pour wine into ice cube trays and freeze. Pop out a cube or two whenever you need a quick addition for cooking.

Cooking with leftover wine is a budget-friendly way to make sure nothing goes to waste.

Wrapping Up

Storing and serving wine doesn't have to be complicated. By paying attention to light, temperature, and proper sealing, you can keep your bottles tasting fresh and vibrant.

When it's time to pour, serving at the right temperature makes a noticeable difference in flavor and aroma. And if you end up with leftovers, you have options—whether that's saving the wine for later drinking or turning it into a delicious addition to your next meal.

In the next chapter, we'll take a journey around the world and explore some of the most famous wine regions, so you can better understand the stories behind the bottles you love.

Chapter 9 – Exploring Wine Regions: Your Virtual Passport

One of the most exciting things about wine is that every bottle tells a story. The grapes, the soil, the climate, and the traditions of the people who make it all come together to create something unique.

Opening a bottle can feel like a little trip around the world without leaving your kitchen table. Maybe you're sipping a crisp Sauvignon Blanc from New Zealand, a bold Cabernet Sauvignon from California, or a delicate Pinot Noir from Burgundy, France.

In this chapter, we'll explore some of the world's most famous wine regions. Think of this as your virtual passport to understanding how geography, culture, and history shape the wines you love. Along the way, we'll share fun facts and suggest a few "bucket list" wines to try at least once.

Old World vs. New World Wines

Before we dive into specific regions, it helps to understand the basic distinction between **Old World** and **New World** wines. These terms don't just refer to geography, they also reflect winemaking philosophies and styles.

Old World Wines

- **Where They're From:** Europe and parts of the Middle East where wine has been made for centuries.
- **Examples:** France, Italy, Spain, Germany, Portugal, Greece.
- **Style:** Typically, more restrained and subtle, with an emphasis on elegance and balance.
- **Focus:** The region and tradition. Labels often highlight where the wine is from rather than the grape variety.

In Short:

Old World wines tend to tell a story of history and place, with subtle flavors that evolve as you sip.

New World Wines

- **Where They're From:** Countries that began making wine more recently (historically speaking).
- **Examples:** United States, Australia, New Zealand, Chile, Argentina, South Africa.
- **Style:** Often bolder, fruit-forward, and more approachable for beginners.
- **Focus:** The grape variety is usually front and center on the label, making it easier for shoppers to know what they're buying.

In Short:

New World wines are generally vibrant, straightforward, and easy to understand, though many have developed their own traditions over time.

France: A Wine Legacy

France is often considered the heart of the wine world, home to some of the most iconic regions and styles. French wines can seem intimidating at first because the labels focus on place names rather than grape varieties, but once you know a few basics, it becomes much easier to navigate.

Bordeaux

- **Famous For:** Red blends featuring Cabernet Sauvignon and Merlot.
- **Style:** Structured, elegant, and built to age.
- **Fun Fact:** The Left Bank of Bordeaux is known for Cabernet-heavy blends, while the Right Bank leans more toward Merlot.
- **Bucket List Wine:** A classic Bordeaux blend from a well-known producer like Château Margaux (splurge-worthy) or a more affordable bottle from a smaller estate.

Burgundy (Bourgogne)

- **Famous For:** Pinot Noir (red) and Chardonnay (white).
- **Style:** Complex, nuanced, and often delicate.
- **Fun Fact:** Burgundy vineyards are divided into tiny plots called "climats," many with centuries of history.
- **Bucket List Wine:** A silky Pinot Noir from the Côte de Nuits or a crisp, minerally Chardonnay from Chablis.

Champagne

- **Famous For:** Sparkling wine made using traditional methods.
- **Style:** Bubbly, refined, and celebratory.
- **Fun Fact:** Only sparkling wine made in the Champagne region can legally be called Champagne.
- **Bucket List Wine:** A true Champagne, whether a splurge-worthy vintage bottle or a more accessible non-vintage Brut.

Italy: Passion and Tradition

Italy is as diverse in wine as it is in food. Nearly every region produces its own styles, often tied closely to local cuisine.

Tuscany

- **Famous For:** Chianti, Super Tuscans, and Brunello di Montalcino.
- **Grape of Choice:** Sangiovese.
- **Style:** Rustic, food-friendly wines with bright acidity and earthy notes.
- **Fun Fact:** Super Tuscans were originally rebellious blends that broke Italian wine laws—and ended up becoming world-famous.
- **Bucket List Wine:** A rich, savory Brunello di Montalcino paired with pasta or roasted meats.

Piedmont

- **Famous For:** Barolo and Barbaresco.
- **Grape of Choice:** Nebbiolo.
- **Style:** Bold, complex, and age-worthy reds with aromas of rose, tar, and dried herbs.
- **Fun Fact:** Barolo is often called the "King of Wines," while Barbaresco is its "Queen."
- **Bucket List Wine:** A well-aged Barolo—ideal for a special occasion.

Spain: Bold and Accessible

Spain offers incredible value and a wide range of styles, from rich reds to festive sparkling wines.

Rioja

- **Famous For:** Tempranillo-based red wines.
- **Style:** Smooth, spicy, and perfect for pairing with hearty dishes.
- **Fun Fact:** Rioja wines are labeled by how long they've been aged—Crianza, Reserva, and Gran Reserva.
- **Bucket List Wine:** A Gran Reserva Rioja for its deep, complex character.

Cava

- **Famous For:** Affordable, high-quality sparkling wines.
- **Style:** Crisp, bubbly, and versatile.
- **Fun Fact:** Cava is made using the same traditional method as Champagne but costs a fraction of the price.
- **Bucket List Wine:** A well-made Brut Cava to celebrate without overspending.

United States: Innovation and Variety

The U.S. wine scene is vibrant and ever evolving, with California leading the way and other states gaining recognition.

California

- **Famous For:** Napa Valley Cabernet Sauvignon, Sonoma Chardonnay, and Zinfandel.
- **Style:** Bold, fruit-forward, and approachable.
- **Fun Fact:** California produces nearly 90% of American wine.
- **Bucket List Wine:** A Napa Valley Cabernet Sauvignon—splurge or save, you'll find fantastic options at every price point.

Oregon

- **Famous For:** Pinot Noir.
- **Style:** Elegant, balanced, and reminiscent of Burgundy, France.
- **Fun Fact:** Oregon's Willamette Valley has a climate similar to Burgundy, making it perfect for Pinot Noir grapes.
- **Bucket List Wine:** A silky, nuanced Pinot Noir from the Willamette Valley.

Washington

- **Famous For:** Merlot, Syrah, and Riesling.
- **Style:** Diverse, offering both bold reds and crisp whites.
- **Fun Fact:** Washington's consistent climate produces reliable, high-quality wines year after year.
- **Bucket List Wine:** A Washington Syrah for its rich, spicy depth.

Other Regions to Explore

While the regions above are some of the most well-known, there are other areas producing exciting wines worth seeking out.

Australia

- **Famous For:** Shiraz (Syrah).
- **Style:** Big, bold reds with ripe fruit flavors and spice.
- **Fun Fact:** Australia's Barossa Valley is one of the world's top Shiraz regions.
- **Bucket List Wine:** A classic Barossa Valley Shiraz.

Chile

- **Famous For:** Cabernet Sauvignon, Carménère, and Sauvignon Blanc.
- **Style:** Affordable, high-quality wines with excellent consistency.
- **Fun Fact:** Carménère was once thought extinct but was rediscovered thriving in Chilean vineyards.
- **Bucket List Wine:** A smooth, earthy Carménère.

South Africa

- **Famous For:** Chenin Blanc and Pinotage.
- **Style:** A mix of Old World elegance and New World boldness.
- **Fun Fact:** Pinotage is a uniquely South African grape, created by crossing Pinot Noir and Cinsaut.
- **Bucket List Wine:** A rich, smoky Pinotage or a crisp Chenin Blanc.

Wrapping It Up: Your Wine Travel Goals

Exploring wines from around the world is like tasting a global story. Each region offers its own traditions, climate, and flavor profiles, giving you endless opportunities to discover something new.

You don't need to buy expensive bottles to enjoy this journey. Even affordable wines can introduce you to the unique characteristics of a place.

Consider making a wine "bucket list" for yourself. Maybe you'll try a classic French Champagne, a bold Australian Shiraz, or a smooth Spanish Rioja. Every new bottle is a step in your adventure.

In the next chapter, we'll shift focus from exploring the world to mastering the moment—how to become a confident wine lover with practical tips for enjoying your wine journey every day.

Chapter 10 – Becoming a Confident Wine Lover

Congratulations! You've come a long way in your wine journey. By now, you've learned how to read labels, taste wine with confidence, pair it with food, store it properly, and even explore wines from around the world.

What started as curiosity may now feel like a genuine passion. This final chapter is all about helping you take the next steps—growing your knowledge, sharing your love of wine with others, and, most importantly, keeping the experience joyful and stress-free.

Wine isn't meant to be a source of pressure or intimidation. It's meant to be savored, celebrated, and shared. Let's talk about how to make wine a lasting part of your life in a way that feels authentic and fun.

Tracking Your Wine Journey

One of the best ways to build confidence is to track your experiences. Think of it like keeping a personal wine diary. This not only helps you remember the bottles you've loved (and the ones you haven't) but also deepens your understanding of your tastes over time.

Wine Journals

A classic wine journal is a simple, low-tech way to record your discoveries.

You can jot down:

- The wine's name, region, and vintage year.
- Where you bought it or tasted it.
- Flavors and aromas you noticed.
- Whether you'd buy it again and what foods you paired it with.

Journaling makes it easier to recognize patterns. Maybe you'll discover that you consistently enjoy Sauvignon Blanc from New Zealand or that Italian reds are your go-to for pasta nights.

Apps for Wine Lovers

If you prefer a digital approach, there are plenty of apps designed to make wine tracking easy.

Most allow you to:

- Scan wine labels with your phone to save details automatically.
- Write notes and rate wines on the go.
- Browse recommendations based on your previous favorites.

Some popular apps even create a virtual cellar for you, keeping track of the bottles you have at home.

Tasting Clubs

Joining a tasting club—either locally or online—is another fun way to grow your knowledge.

- Many clubs host monthly events where members bring a bottle to share and discuss.
- Online clubs can deliver curated wines to your door, giving you new varieties to try without the guesswork.
- Tasting with others helps you hear different perspectives and discover wines you might not have chosen on your own.

Whether you choose a notebook, an app, or a social group, tracking your journey helps you feel like an active participant in the world of wine rather than just a spectator.

Hosting Wine Nights with Friends

Wine is even more enjoyable when shared. Hosting a casual wine night is a great way to bring people together, learn, and laugh without spending a fortune or stressing over the details.

Keep It Simple

You don't need to host an elaborate dinner. A few bottles of wine, some cheese, and a handful of snacks are more than enough. The goal is connection, not perfection.

Suggestions for easy gatherings:

- **Theme Nights:**
  Pick a theme, like "California vs. France" or "Under $15 Finds."
- **Wine and Cheese Party:**
  Pair a few cheeses with different wine styles and let everyone experiment.
- **Blind Tasting Game:**
  Cover bottles with paper bags and see if anyone can guess the varietal or country.

Make It Interactive

Encourage guests to share what they taste and enjoy.

- Provide small note cards for jotting down impressions.
- Remind everyone there are no wrong answers—wine is subjective!
- Celebrate differing opinions; they make the experience richer.

The more you host, the more confident you'll become in selecting and presenting wines.

Exploring More Advanced Concepts

Once you've built a strong foundation, you may feel ready to go deeper into the world of wine. This doesn't mean you have to become an expert overnight, but there's a lot to explore when the time feels right.

Ideas for taking your knowledge further:

- **Learn About Aging Wine:**
  Discover why certain wines improve with time and how to start a small collection.
- **Study Specific Regions:**
  Focus on one country or area at a time to gain a deeper appreciation for its styles and traditions.
- **Take a Class or Workshop:**
  Local wine shops, community colleges, or online courses often offer approachable lessons.
- **Experiment with Food Pairings:**
  Challenge yourself to create meals specifically designed to highlight particular wines.

Think of these steps as continuing education—but without the tests or homework.

Keeping Wine Fun and Approachable

As you grow more knowledgeable, it's easy to slip into a mindset where wine feels serious or even competitive. Don't let that happen.

Wine should always be a source of joy. It's about moments, memories, and the simple pleasure of a shared bottle.

Tips for staying grounded:

- Don't chase prestige labels just to impress others.
- Keep trying new wines, even if they seem unfamiliar or inexpensive.
- Share your favorites with friends rather than hoarding them for "perfect" occasions.
- Remember that taste is personal. What you love is just as valid as anyone else's opinion.

At its heart, wine is meant to bring people together—not create distance or snobbery.

Final Toast: Celebrate Your Progress

Think back to where you were when you opened this book. Maybe you felt intimidated by wine labels or unsure about what to order at a restaurant. Now, you've built the skills to navigate the wine world with ease and confidence.

You've learned to taste thoughtfully, pair creatively, buy wisely, and store carefully. You've explored regions, discovered new favorites, and even found ways to share your passion with others.

So, here's to you. Pour yourself a glass—of anything you enjoy, no rules attached—and raise it high.

Cheers to your journey, your discoveries, and all the delicious sips still to come.

May wine continue to be a source of joy, adventure, and connection in your life for many years to come.

Wrapping Up the Book

Wine is a lifelong adventure. There will always be new bottles to taste, new regions to explore, and new memories to make.

Whether you stay casual or dive deeper, the most important thing is to savor the experience. Keep learning, keep sharing, and, above all, keep having fun.

Because at the end of the day, wine isn't about rules or rituals—it's about the simple joy of raising a glass with the people who matter most.

Glossary of Wine Terms

Wine has its own language, and while it might seem complicated at first, most terms are simpler than they sound. Here's a quick guide to some of the words you've encountered throughout this book.

- **Acidity:** The crisp, refreshing quality that makes wine feel lively on your tongue.
- **Aging:** The process of letting wine develop over time, either in barrels or bottles, to enhance flavor and complexity.
- **Appellation:** A specific geographic area where wine is produced, often with rules about grape types and methods.
- **Aroma:** The smell of the wine, especially before you take a sip.
- **Balance:** When no single flavor overpowers another, everything works together harmoniously.
- **Body:** How the wine feels in your mouth. Light-bodied wines are delicate, while full-bodied wines feel richer and heavier.
- **Brut:** A term used to describe very dry sparkling wine.
- **Decanting:** Pouring wine from the bottle into another vessel to let it "breathe" and open its flavors.
- **Dry:** A wine with little to no residual sugar. It doesn't taste sweet.
- **Finish:** The lingering taste that stays in your mouth after swallowing.

- **Legs:** Streaks of wine that run down the inside of the glass after swirling—more about alcohol or sugar content than quality.
- **Mouthfeel:** The texture of the wine, such as silky, crisp, or velvety.
- **Notes:** Flavors or aromas detected in the wine, like fruit, spice, or floral hints.
- **Reserve:** Traditionally meant a higher-quality wine aged longer before release, though today it can also be a marketing term.
- **Tannins:** Compounds from grape skins and seeds that add bitterness, dryness, or structure to red wines.
- **Terroir:** The unique combination of soil, climate, and location that influences a wine's character.
- **Vintage:** The year the grapes were harvested, listed on the bottle.
- **Varietal:** The type of grape used to make the wine, like Cabernet Sauvignon or Chardonnay.

Quick Tasting Sheet Guide

While we don't include printable templates, here's a simple framework you can use to jot down tasting notes in a notebook or on your phone whenever you try a new wine.

What to Record:

- **Wine Name & Vintage:** Example: 2020 Napa Valley Chardonnay
- **Region:** Where the grapes were grown.
- **Appearance:** Color and clarity.
- **Aroma:** First impressions when you smell the wine.
- **Flavor:** Key flavors you taste—fruity, earthy, spicy, floral, etc.
- **Body & Texture:** Light, medium, or full-bodied; smooth, silky, crisp.
- **Overall Impression:** Did you enjoy it? Would you buy it again?
- **Pairing Notes:** Foods you tried it with and how well it worked.

Using this method over time will help you remember your favorites and better understand your personal preferences.

Quick Reference Pairing Chart

Here's an easy reference for matching common wines with everyday foods. Think of it as your go-to cheat sheet when planning meals.

Food	Best Wine Matches	Why It Works
Pizza	Merlot, Chianti, Zinfandel	Tomato sauce loves fruity, medium-bodied reds.
Burgers	Cabernet Sauvignon, Syrah/Shiraz	Bold wines match hearty flavors.
Pasta	Pinot Noir, Chardonnay	Versatile for both creamy and tomato sauces.
Cheese Plate	Sparkling Wine, Sauvignon Blanc, Pinot Noir	Acidity and bubbles balance creamy textures.
Grilled Vegetables	Rosé, Pinot Grigio	Light, fresh wines highlight veggie flavors.
Spicy Foods	Riesling, Moscato, Rosé	Slight sweetness cools the heat.
Seafood	Sauvignon Blanc, Pinot Grigio, Sparkling Wine	Crisp wines keep seafood tasting fresh.
Steak or Lamb	Cabernet Sauvignon, Malbec, Syrah	Big reds complement rich meats.

Resources & Further Reading

If you've caught the wine bug and want to keep learning, here are some great places to continue your journey.

Books

- *Wine Folly: Magnum Edition* by Madeline Puckette and Justin Hammack – A beautifully illustrated, beginner-friendly guide.
- *The Wine Bible* by Karen MacNeil – A comprehensive yet approachable resource.
- *Adventures on the Wine Route* by Kermit Lynch – A travelogue through some of Europe's most famous wine regions.

Websites

- **Wine Folly** – www.winefolly.com – Excellent for quick tips and visual guides.
- **VinePair** – www.vinepair.com – Articles, reviews, and fun wine quizzes.
- **Wine Spectator** – www.winespectator.com – For ratings, news, and expert advice.

Apps

- **Vivino:** Scan labels, track your favorites, and read reviews from other wine lovers.
- **CellarTracker:** Great for managing a personal wine collection.
- **Delectable:** A social platform for discovering and rating wines.

About the Author

Ava Vintner believes wine should be fun, approachable, and free of unnecessary snobbery. After years of wandering wine shops, tasting rooms, and farmers' markets, she realized that many beginners felt intimidated by the world of wine.

Her mission became clear: to demystify wine and help people enjoy it on their own terms.

When she's not sipping and writing, Ava loves hosting casual wine nights with friends, traveling to explore new wine regions, and experimenting with creative food pairings in her cozy kitchen. She's living proof that you don't need a degree or a cellar full of expensive bottles to be a true wine lover, you just need curiosity and a corkscrew.

Favorite everyday wine:

A crisp Sauvignon Blanc paired with a good book and a sunny afternoon.

Index

The index helps you quickly find key topics covered in the book.

A

Acidity, 162

Aging, 158

Appellation, 160

B

Balance, 163

Barolo, 108

Bordeaux, 104

Brut, 111

C

Cabernet Sauvignon, 76

Cava, 115

Chianti, 108

Cork storage, 140

F

Food pairings, 92

Fortified wine, 142

France, 102

P

Pinot Grigio, 84

Pinot Noir, 74

Port, 142

Prosecco, 112

R

Red wine basics, 70

Riesling, 82

Rosé, 86

S

Sauvignon Blanc, 80

Sparkling wine, 110

Storage tips, 138

Syrah/Shiraz, 78

T

Tannins, 164

Terroir, 65

Tuscany, 108

W

Washington wines, 118

Wine clubs, 130

Wine terms glossary, 158

A Final Note

Thank you for joining this journey through the wonderful world of wine.

Whether you're sipping an inexpensive weeknight bottle or celebrating with something truly special, remember wine is about enjoyment, not perfection.

Here's to raising a glass, sharing laughter, and making memories—one sip at a time. **Cheers!**

Printed in Dunstable, United Kingdom